The #1 Guide To Outsourcing

Outsourcing
Entrepreneur

I0486141

Build Your Online Business By
Outsourcing With Freelancers
& Virtual Assistants!

James Harper

STOP!!! Before you read any further....Would you like to know the Success Secrets of how to make Passive Income Online?

If your answer is yes, then you are not alone. Thousands of people are looking for the secret to learning how to create their own online passive income style business.

If you have been searching for these answers without much luck, you are in the right place!

Because I want to make sure to give you as much value as possible for purchasing this book, right now for a limited time you can get 3 incredible bonuses for free.

At the end of this book I describe all 3 bonuses. You can access them at the end. But for those of you that want to grab your bonuses right now. See below.

<u>**Just Go Here For Free Instant Access:**</u>

<u>**www.OperationAwesomeLife.com/FreeBonuses**</u>

Legal Notice

Disclaimer Notice

Table Of Contents

Introduction

I want to thank you and congratulate you for purchasing the book, *"The Outsourcing Entrepreneur: The #1 Guide To Building Your Online Business By Outsourcing With Freelancers"*.

This book contains proven steps and strategies on how to build an online business empire outsourcing with virtual assistants and freelancers. This book is a fully comprehensive resource on the subject of outsourcing and will not only provide you with the sources of where to find the best freelancers, but also with possible online business ideas that will work well with outsourcing.

Thanks again for purchasing this book, I hope you enjoy it!

Chapter 1: What Is Outsourcing?

In order to thrive in their industry, there are times when businesses would need to hire people outside their organization to accomplish specialized tasks. This process is known as "outsourcing". Basically, it is the strategic use of resources from the outside to complete tasks or assignments that are traditionally managed by internal staff. Major functions are often outsourced to specialized service providers as an attempt to make the business process more efficient.

In its early days, the most common reason for outsourcing is cost reduction. Today, however, it is often done as a strategy to maximize the internal staff's skills and expertise for carrying out core-value tasks. More often than not, it is more cost-effective to hire specialists to get the job done than to spend time and money training company staff for it. Some other reasons for outsourcing include:

- Improvement of the company's focus
- Insufficient internal resources
- The need for efficiency when it comes to time-intensive and specialized tasks
- Internal staff is needed for other purposes
- Risk-sharing with an affiliate company

Of course, there are also considerations when it comes to outsourcing critical tasks. In order for outsourcing to be successful, there must be:

- An understanding of the company's objectives and goals
- A strategic plan and a long-term vision
- A contract that is well-structured
- Involvement and support from the senior executives
- Open communications with the involved groups
- Proper management of business relationships

These days, there are many services that can be obtained through outsourcing. This is because outsourcing has become a widespread business and the demand for it is expected to remain constant as long as companies continue to expand and strive for excellence. Some of the outsourced services include:

- Call centers
- Virtual assistants
- Consultancy
- Advertising
- Records and purchasing
- Bookkeeping and payroll
- Field service dispatch
- Food services
- Building maintenance
- Fleet services
- Security services

If you are already running an online business, or are just planning to start one, it is highly advisable to learn more about outsourcing. Nowadays, outsourcing has certainly changed the way people do business –– business owners no longer need to invest in office space, human resource managers, and time for training their employees for specific tasks. Hiring an expert from the outside is all they need to get a job done.

Getting Started with Outsourcing

Before you outsource a particular task to a freelancer, it is important to first define the scope of the task to be accomplished beforehand. Having your project details readily posted will make it easier for interested applicants to gauge if they can provide you the service that you need. At the same time, this will make it easier for you to figure out who is the best candidate for the job.

The right legal requirements are also essential in closing the best outsourcing deal. When it comes down to contract signing, it is important for all the details to be clear and fair, with all negotiations straightened out from the very start. It must include the complete scope of the services to be rendered by the freelancer or service provider. These are what are usually referred to as "service levels" and "service level agreements".

Service levels are the target tasks agreed upon by the client and the service provider. The list can be short or long depending on what the client requires. Detailed schedules must be established such that neither party can be in doubt of what needs to be accomplished by the hired service provider. In addition to describing the expectations and deliverables, a good agreement must also state the reporting methods for proper service level assessment. This could also include benefits and sanctions every time the requirements are met or not.

Basically, the major consideration when it comes to outsourcing with service levels is the clarity of the contract. However, problems may be encountered if the contract covers many tasks requiring various levels of functions and services. For this reason, objectivity and open communications is very important to ensure that service levels are fair for both the client and the service provider.

Chapter 2: Some Examples Of Online Freelance Jobs

People who are looking for opportunities to earn extra income are probably already familiar with the term, "freelancing". A freelancer or a freelance worker is someone who is self-employed, performing specialized tasks for one or more employers. His or her commitment to a particular employer only goes as long as what is stated in the service level agreement. Freelancers can sometimes be represented by an agency or a company that resells their services, while others are totally independent.

These workers may choose to work part-time or full-time depending on their preference. Usually they go by their task on their own terms –– without any strict guidelines –– as long as they are able to deliver the work according to the client's provisions. Freelancers who offer services to the same employer for a longer period than usual may sometimes be considered as "permalancers", or "permanent freelancers". However, being a permalancer does not necessarily guarantee added benefits just as a normal employee would have when he stays for a certain amount of time with his company.

Those who wish to earn extra money on the side or those who want to work their own way without strict schedules should definitely look into freelancing. It is one of the easiest, quickest, and most cost-effective ways to start honing your skills and working for yourself. On the other hand, if you are someone who thinks of starting an online business, knowing some of the online freelance jobs available may give you an idea on the type of business that you should pursue.

Writers

Freelance writing may take a lot of work, but the good thing about it is that no special tool or equipment is needed to get started. You don't need to write like a distinguished author in order to get projects, but your writing has to have minimal grammatical errors and coherent structure at the very least.

Translators

Being fluent in a second language gives you a great opportunity to do some freelance work. There will be some variation in fees depending on the language that you are able to translate. However, one of the major things that can affect freelance translation fees is whether you have a certification from the American Translators Association or not. Those who are certified can expect to earn $72,000 per year, while those who are not will earn an average of $53,000 per year.

SEO (Search Engine Optimization) Experts

Some top-of-the-line SEO experts will charge $1,000 per hour for their SEO works and assessments. High-end freelancers, on the other hand, usually charge $300 to $500 per hour. Those who are relatively new to the field can get the job for $50 per hour as long as they have the necessary skills to do the work. Entry-level rates may be significantly lower than the rates of more experienced SEO freelancers, but this is because entry-level jobs generally follow simpler steps when it comes to optimizing websites for search engines.

Social Media Marketers

Before, social media wasn't much of a tool when it comes to establishing online presence. Today, however, using social media together with your online business can bring you not only the website traffic that you want but the sales that you've been aiming for as well. Knowing the ins and outs of social media marketing can make a newcomer earn $15 per hour, but those who have proven track records may charge up to $250 per hour. Of course, experience is not the only thing that can guarantee high payment rates. You also need to work closely with high-paying businesses that don't already have a social media department.

Mobile Developers

The advent of smart phones has made the business of mobile app development very in demand today. This means that mobile developers will not run out of projects anytime soon. If you get a chance to work with big-shot corporate clients, you can earn more than $100,000 for developing a single app for them. Of course, the complexity of the project is also a factor.

Online freelance jobs are not limited to the aforementioned tasks. If you are on the creative side, you can also get freelance projects as an illustrator, graphic artist, videographer, voice over actor, musician, etc. Having creative and analytical skills will definitely help you land a great job as a freelancer. The best thing is, finding the right clients can make freelance work even more rewarding than a day job.

Chapter 3: Building An Online Business With Freelancers

Now that you have decided to start an online business, one of the options that you are probably looking into to get it up and running is to hire freelancers. That is not really an unusual move, and in fact many starters turn to freelancers for help. This is because hiring a freelancer is regarded as an efficient and practical solution –– if you hire the right person, you can get the same good results as a reputable company can produce for a smaller fee.

We already know that all businesses start with a plan, and more often than not the first step is the hardest one to execute. Starting a business, whether it's online or offline, requires a lot of time, decisions, and investments. Failing to make the right decisions will not only prove to be a waste of money but a waste of all your efforts as well. But how do you ensure that your business will thrive and succeed?

Starting a Business with Freelancers

Let us take the web design process as an example. Hiring a web agency to work on the web design and development process will cost around $2,000. This amount is apart from the cost of SEO and content creation, which is another $1,800 combined. So the approximate amount of all this work is $3,800 when you opt to hire a web agency to do it for you.

Hiring freelancers, on the other hand, will cost you much less than that. You may opt to post two projects on a trusted website for hiring freelancers, such as Freelancer.com: one is for the web design and development and the other one is for content writing and SEO. Outsourcing these tasks to a freelancer will cost you only around $1,800 –– that is $2,000 less than what you have to pay if you choose to give this job to a web agency. To ensure that you will be getting high-quality results, you can always check the freelancers' portfolios before agreeing to assign the project to them.

Ensuring High-Quality Results

It's always a good idea to ensure that a good business relationship will be established between you and the freelancer that you're about to hire. Even though you intend to hire on a per project basis only, it's better to have someone to contact that already has proven results. Here are some of the things that you can do to maintain good relationships with freelancers:

- Motivate them.

   One of the reasons why many people choose to hire freelancers is because their service is inexpensive compared to agencies. However, they do the same amount of work and effort as their employed counterparts. If you've always been impressed with their results and you want them to work for you for your other projects, it is a good idea to give them incentives once in a while. This will give your freelancer the idea that you value their skills, proving that they are an asset to you.

- Pay them on time.

   No one likes being paid late for delivering high-quality results on time. Paying freelancers on time encourages them to be more dedicated to their job, and it will also put you in their list of good employers. Be fair and give credit where credit is due.

- Believe in what they can do.

Just because freelancers charge less does not mean that their outputs are of less quality. When you choose to hire a particular freelancer for a project, it is not a good idea to be all frantic and question them so much about whether they can do the job or not. It might be hard to trust someone new at first but that's exactly what feedbacks and portfolios are for. When you browse through their portfolio and read through their feedback, believe in what you see and read and mostly, believe that they can also do the job for you.

Outsourcing Freelancers

The key to starting an online business is making sure what your interests are. Sure, you can try just about anything, but working on something you really like will add a different kind of flare to the way you do things. If you have no clear focus as of yet, you have keep it simple at the start. It should be something that requires little money and technical expertise, and it should be easy to manage with a proven track record of success, even for beginners. Of course, it has to be
something that doesn't bore you.

If you are ready to get started, here are some options:

1. **Information Marketing**

   At this point in human history the demand for information is constantly increasing due to the convenience in which it can be retrieved. If you have particular hobbies or if you are particularly interested in an odd topic, you can actually make money out of it. More than 90% of people go online to seek for answers, and you can give them what they need in exchange for some cash. Once you have established your niche, it is a good idea to outsource content writing to freelancers to ensure that you always have new topics at your chosen schedule.

2. **Remote Technical Support or Virtual Assistant**

A lot of small businesses don't have the funds and resources for an in-house IT employee, so when they encounter technical problems what they usually do is call a trusted friend or family member who's good with computers. However, help from such people cannot always be guaranteed. If you have an online store or you offer your services via a website, it is recommended to outsource a technical support personnel or virtual assistant to ensure that all technical problems will be immediately fixed.

Now that you know how you can build a business with freelancers on board, the next chapter shall discuss the benefits and pitfalls of outsourcing.

Chapter 4: The Pitfalls Of Outsourcing

Businesses will always look for ways to cut down expenses to gain more profit. In the first chapter, we discussed how outsourcing is often the chosen strategy to reduce labor costs. While hiring freelancers presents a lot of benefits, such as cheaper labor and fresh ideas from outside the company, working with freelancers also has some pitfalls.

Limited Skills Assessment

When you hire a freelancer for a project, you usually pick someone who you think is the most fit for the job until you find out that they lack the skills that you are really looking for. While some are fortunate enough to hire someone who can really do the task, some end up with a freelance worker who is not qualified. This happens because there is little chance for you to truly assess an applicant –– the interviews are not done in person, and the traditional checks and balances upon application are also not there. Aside from looking at their ratings and portfolio, you can try asking them to create a sample work for your project before handing them the entire job.

Longer Response Time

Freelancers are often offshore, and this immediately limits how you can oversee their work progress. When they say that they had worked on your project for a specific number of hours, more or less you will just have to believe what they're saying. This can be problematic when you're paying the freelancer by the hour and not by a flat rate. Being a number of time zones apart is also troublesome when you need to request some modifications. Fortunately, programs like Skype make it easier to handle such problems.

Worker Loyalty

When a company hires someone to work for them, the employee understands that he must be committed to the company for an indefinite time. His full attention is only with the company during working hours. Freelancers, on the other hand, can commit only when they choose to. Sometimes there is a tendency for them to even abandon projects when they are not obligated by contracts. As free agents, freelancers also often handle several projects at once and you may not always have their undivided attention.

Chapter 5: Finding Freelancers Online

For big businesses, it is not surprising if they need to hire full-time employees that need to be more hands-on with their tasks. For smaller businesses, however, work can be done much faster and more efficiently when it is outsourced to a freelancer. Most services offer agree to complete the job through a contract, and they also handle the tax services as well. Here are some websites where you can find freelancers:

1. **Elance**

    Most jobs at Elance cost $20 per hour or more, and the job specialties range from C++ programming, data science, multimedia and design, writing, finance management, translation, customer service, engineering and architecture, writing, and web development. They also have a business solutions package for those who are already managing a variety of contractors. The website lets you automate invoice and payments, making it easier to track down your labor costs.

2. **oDesk**

    oDesk's pool of top freelancers include logo designers, website developers, article writers, SEO specialists, personal assistants, and WordPress experts. Their website is pretty easy to navigate and its contractor management tools are also very detailed. If you are only want applicants who have already proven themselves then you can keep a job posting private and visible only to those users that you have invited.

3. **Freelancer.com**

Freelancer.com is one of the biggest outsourcing venues for small businesses. They have a wide range of projects, from local jobs and trades, business and accounting, human resources, translations, marketing and sales, product sourcing, science and engineering, data entry, content writing, and information technology. Its community has over 9 million users from more than 200 countries all over the world. You can also post contests for your projects if you need fresh ideas.

4. Guru

The most popular freelance jobs that you can find in Guru include websites and e-commerce jobs, e-mail designs, programming and databases, engineering and CAD, networking and telephone systems, illustration and art, broadcasting, admin support, fashion and interior designs, photography and videography, and telemarketing. It is similar to oDesk and Elance but on a smaller scale.

5. Task Rabbit

Task Rabbit offers a great concept in the world of online freelancing. While other websites focus on offshore workers, Task Rabbit focuses on people who will offer freelance work within your local area. Task Rabbit's database works such that they match your task specifications with someone who just lives nearby. However, the downside of Task Rabbit is that it only available in limited locations as of the moment.

It may be overwhelming to sort through all the available freelancers at first as surely there will be many options to choose from. Hiring the best freelancer for a particular job definitely takes some effort, but it is better to take your time and be keen than just pick whoever is convenient. If you are to invest in the services of independent contractors for your online business, you have to make sure that they are worth it.

Conclusion

Thank you again for purchasing this book on outsourcing your business for massive success!

I am extremely excited to pass this information along to you, and I am so happy that you now have read and can hopefully implement these strategies to execute your plans.

I hope this book was able to help you better understand the way freelancing and outsourcing works. Also, if you know of anyone else that could benefit from the information presented here, please let them know about this book and share what you have learned.

The next step is to create and fulfill your online business plans and find the freelancers that will help you succeed!

Finally, if you enjoyed this book and feel it has added value to your life in any way, please take the time to share your thoughts and post a review on Amazon. It'd be greatly appreciated!

Thank you and good luck!

Preview Of:

<u>Hot Small Business Ideas!</u>

25 Smokin' Hot Start Up Business Ideas To Spark You Entrepreneurship Creativity And Have You In Business Fast!

Introduction

I want to thank you and congratulate you for purchasing the book, *"Entrepreneurship Ideas Now!: 25 Smokin' Hot Start Up Business Ideas To Spark Your Entrepreneurship Creativity And Have You In Business Fast!"*.

This book contains 25 proven small business ideas to find the right niche for you to become successful.

Congratulations on making the first step towards a better life for yourself and your loved ones. Creating a business is the financially smartest thing you can do in today's often volatile job market. As more and more folks get laid off in the rapidly changing economy we live in, more and more people are looking for a more stable source of income in which they have better control of.

I could go on and on about the benefits of owning and operating your own business, but I won't because that's not why you are here. You already know you want to own your own business and make your own decisions; you just need to know where to channel your drive and hard work. In this book you will find 25 of the Hottest Small Business Ideas for today!

One thing I have learned over the years of being an entrepreneur is that if you don't have passion for the business you are in - then you most likely will not make it. I'm here to fuel that passion by giving you some great ideas you can really sink your teeth into.

Thanks again for purchasing this book, I hope you enjoy it!

Chapter 1: Starting Your Own Online Business

Nobody gets rich by remaining an employee forever. You need to take greater risks, invest and be your own boss to earn more and provide a much better life for yourself and your family. That is practically how your bosses does it.

There is no better time to start a small business than now. Marketing has never been easier, thanks to the multitude of channels, tools and online facilities that help you have success in marketing without spending a dime. The awareness in business management is also higher, so you will have more time and opportunities to thrive in your chosen industry and make a name for yourself.

Starting your own business is not just about the extra income; it is about the extra time for yourself and your family, and all the comfortable and luxurious perks that come with it. Starting your own smoking hot business is your ultimate ticket to better living, having all resources to buy whatever you want and plan ahead without having to consider vacation/leave credits, office schedules and unrelenting superiors.

Being your own boss is a life-changing decision that can steer your whole life – upwards if you have the dedication and willingness to learn and develop your craft, or downwards if you cannot commit to your decision.

For a starter, you will be introduced to the hottest online businesses you can possibly start.

1. Amazon Affiliate

Affiliate programs are smoking hot; double that for Amazon. This is the new version of product consignment, only done online. You will need to do the marketing, promotions and reviews preferably in the form of blogging to get more customers for Amazon's listed products. This is a fulltime online business with unlimited earning opportunities.

Pros:

- *Famous* – Amazon is the top online shopping site all around the world. The name sells in itself. The program is reliable and has been around for more than a decade now. It is definitely the most trusted affiliate program today.

- *Flexible time* – All the marketing efforts and website setups are all in your good time. You can keep earning while sleeping, so management is not stressful.

- *Low-cost* – Your only expense is the domain and server, although there
are free providers you can choose from.

Cons:

- *Might take time to pick up* – Gaining huge online traffic and website contents may take time, perhaps months before you can actually earn. The good thing is that when it picks up, there is no stopping it.

- *Requires intense internet marketing know-how* – Millions of people all around the world do marketing online. If you want to standout, you need to master the techniques and learn continuously.

2. Niche Blogging

Blogging doesn't run out of steam, and it continues to be the new newspaper, magazine, paperback, diary and variety show. According to Yahoo, the blogging industry recorded its highest revenue in 2013, and there is no sign of backing down anytime soon. Average niche bloggers earn anywhere from $1,000 to $15,000 a month, the latter implying the full-timers.

Pros:

- *Unlimited source of income* – You can earn from ad vendors, paid advertising, PPC, paid publicity and promotions, affiliate programs and dozens more of innovative online opportunities.

- *Easy to set up* – You only need to have flair in writing – informing and entertaining at the same time. Setting up your blog is easy and in fact, you can have it for free. Just pick a topic and niche market you want to tap, and be the best in it.

Cons:

- *Traffic problems* – Online traffic can be a big problem if you will only focus on the actual blogging part. Remember that this is a business; thus, it involves intense marketing and customer relations.

- *Requires patience* – You can't write and have thousands of readers right away. Even the most successful bloggers today needed to build their fan-base over time.

3. SEO Firm

SEO (search engine optimization) is the life of websites, both non-profit and commercial. SEO dictates the competition. It doesn't run out of market. Your business' goal here is to get clients on top of search engines and get them the traffic and conversion that they are targeting. If you have advance knowledge in web and graphic designing, SEO writing, SEM (search engine marketing) and internet marketing strategies, you are ready to get some clients and build websites for them. A team of five specialists is already enough to handle a pool of business websites.

Pros:

- *Easy to set up* – What you do when you make your own website or blog is the same thing you will do for your clients. You might just need support staff for the other technical aspects and to finish projects on deadlines.

- *Low-cost* – Most likely, you already have a usable computer. You only need to buy different software (you can get them for free if you are adept in online sourcing) and additional computers – perhaps rent a server.

- *Easy to market* – Your body of work speaks for itself. The market is unlimited, and your efficiency in the job will dictate how far you can get in the industry.

- *Tough competition* – At the end of the day, your client's online success (in terms of traffic generation, search engine ranking, etc.) will gauge your reputation. There is only one page to aim at but, there are thousands of websites competing. The competition is not only between you and other SEO firms. You need to remember that your client's stand in the competition is also your responsibility.

4. Graphic Designing

You can launch this business as a part of SEO services for company websites and professional bloggers. However, a graphic designing company can also stand alone as it really was before SEO became the buzz. If you are adept in designing, working on your own shouldn't be a problem at all.

You can cater to bloggers and social media addicts who want to take their accounts to another level (many Facebook-ers and Youtube-ers hire graphic and video designers and editors to professionalize their accounts). You can also cater to special occasions, such as weddings, birthday parties, launchings, etc.

Pros:

- *Wide, unlimited market* – Graphic designing services have been here even
   before they were integrated with SEO. Specifically, those who hire graphic

- designers belong to small-scale businesses and private individuals. Your own talent will be your own setback.

- *Low startup cost* – You need a piece of computer, internet connection, printer and a whole lot of creative ingenuity. Depending on the volume of your clientele, you can expand in resources as you expand in operation.

Cons:

- *Professionally limiting* – Many experts believe that graphic designing should just be the beginning of a more expansive business because this alone is very limiting, professional at least. There's not exactly a next level, unless you include other services and provide tangible products as well, such as selling your own souvenir items or expanding to other SEO services as well.

5. eBook Self-Publication

Book and eBook writing are both professions, but self-publication of eBooks is a business. It involves end-to-end processes, from the writing to editing, cover designing to online publication, and marketing to selling. Many bloggers have already shifted to fulltime eBook self-publication as the potential income is higher.

Amazon and Barnes and Noble are the two top online destinations when it comes to eBook publication. You will likely receive just a percentage of the eBook price, but the accumulated earnings are enough to top your monthly income from a fulltime office job. Selling through your own website is also a lucrative idea, but only if you attract huge online traffic and has already set yourself as one of the leaders in your niche industry.

Pros:

- *Unlimited earning potential* – As of 2012, eBook sales have already surpassed hardcover sales, but only next to paperback sales. In the next five to 10 years, it is expected that online publication will be the most marketable form of publication.

- *A potential launch pad to stardom* – This business is not only about the money – millions of money. It is also about legacy, name and popularity.

- *Easy to execute* – Writing shouldn't be a problem. Most of your efforts will go to the cover design and marketing strategies.

Cons:

- *Needs decent online presence* – If you will market your own eBooks, you need to have an existing market-base. Otherwise, starting from scratch will take time to convert into sales.

- *Possible failure* – The failure in the self-publication industry is really high. Many eBook writers don't even crack the 200-sales threshold. If you think your writing skills and creativity are not enough to make a name for yourself, better choose another business.

6. eBay Trading

eBay is the best channel to start a trading business because all types of products are allowed, both new and used. The site is famous for its cheap finds, so pulling a chunk of the market should not be a problem.

You can source out your products from wholesalers, abroad, garage sales, or you can restore old items to make them new.

Pros:

- *High traffic volume* – Six out of 10 internet users have bought an item from eBay. That is how often eBay makes a sales, which means that market is far from being saturated anytime soon.

- *Easy to set up* – When you already have products to sell, you only need a camera, computer and basic knowledge in setting up an eBay account. You can do your own internet marketing, but eBay is already an established shopping destination. Customers go to the site without prodding.

- *Low startup cost* – Depending on your items, your capital can be as low as a couple of hundreds of dollars. It doesn't matter if you sell second-hand items.

Cons:

- *Difficulty with logistics* – This shouldn't really be a problem because dealing with forwarding and logistic company, both local and international, is now simpler.

Nonetheless, you need to take care of it as well, which means extra work.

7. Content Creating

Others call it SEO and technical writing, but content writing is more than just a single component of a fulltime SEO firm. Content writing is less focused on internet marketing stuff – just plain quality content. In the 90s, content writing referred to the outsourced company magazine contents, that included internal newsletters, free magazine giveaways (as a part of store promos) and local ads.

Today, content writing primarily refers to website and blog writing, mostly of private organizations that use their websites not as primary marketing channels but as information centers (which is true for most consumer products that do not really sell online).

Pros:

- *High expected revenue* – Yahoo considers content writing as one of the biggest profession for the next 50 years, especially now that everything is shifting to online publication. The revenue and market are likely to expand without stopping.

- *Simple organizational structure* – A small content writing business doesn't even need to have an office. Most similar companies pool writers online and have them work in virtual offices. You can even do it by yourself if you will take one client at a time.

Cons:

- *Quality concerns* – For a bigger clientele, quality control might be a problem, especially when you do not have in-house editors to help you do quality control, proofreading and copyediting.

8. Server Management

Buying a dedicated server is not something that many small businesses can afford or are even willing to invest in. Server management companies then buy a server space and have it leased out to small companies. You can also have your own server and have it rented as shared server to several clients.

In addition, you must offer support and website management services.

Pros:

- *Huge ROI* – Leasing out a server alone may not incur impressive income, but because of the additional services, you can place a huge premium on top.
- *Huge market-base* – This is a very timely business, so relevant in today's business environment that will not run out of prospective clients in the next few years.

Cons:

- *Requires technical expertise* – Basic knowledge in server management is not enough. You need to have advance skills to make sure that your services are on top.

- *Limited clients* – The size of your clientele will depend on the size of your server.

Thanks for Previewing My Exciting Book Entitled:

"Hot Small Business Ideas! 25 Smokin' Hot Start Up Business Ideas To Spark You Entrepreneurship Creativity And Have You In Business Fast!"

To purchase this book, simply go to the Amazon Kindle store and simply search:

"SMALL BUSINESS IDEAS"

Then just scroll down until you see my book. You will know it is mine because you will see my name "James Harper" underneath the title.

Alternatively, you can visit my author page on Amazon to see this book and other work I have done. Thanks so much, and please don't forget your free bonuses

DON'T LEAVE YET! - CHECK OUT YOUR FREE BONUSES BELOW!

Free Bonus Offer 1: Get Free Access To The OperationAwesomeLife.com VIP Newsletter!

Free Bonus Offer 2: Get A Free Download Of My Friends Amazing Book "Passive Income" First Chapter!

Free Bonus Offer 3: Get A Free Email Series On Making Money Online When You Join Newsletter!

GET ALL 3 FREE

Once you enter your email address you will immediately get free access to this awesome **VIP NEWSLETTER!**

For a limited time, if you join for free right now, you will also get free access to the first chapter of the awesome book "**PASSIVE INCOME**"!

And, last but definitely not least, if you join the newsletter right now, you also will get a free 10 part email series on **10 SUCCESS SECRETS OF MAKING MONEY ONLINE!**

To claim all 3 of your FREE BONUSES just click below!

Just Go Here for all 3 VIP bonuses!

OperationAwesomeLife.com